The **Kodak Book** of

FAST & EASY
SCRAPBOOK PAGES

Lisa Turley

The **Kodak Book** of

FAST & EASY
SCRAPBOOK PAGES

Kerry Arquette & Andrea Zocchi

Published by Lark Books
A Division of Sterling Publishing Co., Inc.
New York

Book Concept and Design: Cantata Books Inc. www.cantatabooks.com
Executive Editor: Kerry Arquette
Editor: Darlene D'Agostino
Copy Editor: Dena Twinem
Cover Design and Art Direction: Andrea Zocchi
Designer: Susha Roberts

    Library of Congress Cataloging-in-Publication Data

Arquette, Kerry.
  The Kodak book of fast & easy scrapbook pages : easy & fun techniques for
beautiful scrapbook pages / Kerry Arquette & Andrea Zocchi. -- 1st ed.
      p. cm.
  Includes index.
  ISBN 1-57990-965-5 (pbk.)
  1. Photograph albums. 2. Photographs--Conservation and restoration. 3.
Scrapbooks. I. Zocchi, Andrea. II. Title. III. Title: Kodak book of fast
and easy scrapbook pages.
  TR501.A76465 2007
  745.593--dc22
                        2006020565

10 9 8 7 6 5 4 3 2 1

First Edition

Published by Lark Books, A Division of Sterling Publishing Co., Inc.
387 Park Avenue South, New York, N.Y. 10016

© 2007, Eastman Kodak Company
Illustrations © Cantata Books Inc.

Distributed in Canada by Sterling Publishing,
c/o Canadian Manda Group, 165 Dufferin Street, Toronto, Ontario, Canada M6K 3H6

Distributed in the United Kingdom by GMC Distribution Services,
Castle Place, 166 High Street, Lewes, East Sussex, England BN7 1XU

Distributed in Australia by Capricorn Link (Australia) Pty Ltd., P.O. Box 704, Windsor, NSW 2756 Australia

Kodak and trade dress are trademarks of Kodak used by Lark Books under trademark license.

Kodak
LICENSED PRODUCT

If you have questions or comments about this book, please contact:
Lark Books
67 Broadway
Asheville, NC 28801
(828) 253-0467

Manufactured in China

ISBN 13: 978-1-57990-965-9
ISBN 10: 1-57990-965-5

For information about custom editions, special sales, premium and corporate purchases, please contact Sterling Special Sales Department at 800-805-5489 or specialsales@sterlingpub.com.

Table of Contents

Start Scrapbooking Today. 6

The Tools of the Trade 7

Design Pointers 8

Organization Tips. 9

Scrapbooking With One Photo   10

Fill 'er With a Photo: Make the most of one large image   12

Divide and Conquer: Fill half your page
with a terrific image 14

*Fast and Easy Color Blocking:
Use paper blocks to create intriguing backgrounds.* 16

Greet a Photo With a Welcoming Mat:
Mat a single photo to give it weight. 18

Being Framed Is a Good Thing: Frame your
photo uniquely 20

Pump Up Your Photo With Patterns: Have fun with
patterned papers 22

Consider a Different Point-of-View: Vary your photo
angles for super strong layouts 24

*Fast and Easy Stamping: A few stamps and inks equal
hundreds of layout possibilities* 26

Embrace the White Space: Have fun scrapbooking on
clean white backgrounds. 28

Clear Away the Clutter: Set your photo on simple,
sleek backgrounds. 30

Juggle a Photo With Colorful Paper Shapes: Use pretty
paper to draw attention to your photo. 32

*Fast and Easy Heat Embossing: Who thought that
heated powder could be so cool?.* 34

Focus on the Face: Use a close-up of your subject for
personality pages. 36

Seize the Moment with a Tight Crop: Move in close,
close, closer for terrific photos. 38

Stretch Creative Impact With Panoramas: Go wide or
long to capture more landscape. 40

Scrapbooking With Two Photos   42

Equal Rights: Scrapbook photos of the same size. 44

The Large and Small of It: Scrapbook with photos of
different sizes 46

What Are You Looking At?: Combine photos that show
who is looking at what 48

Balancing Act: Add poise to your page with a title 50

Find Balance in a Journaling Block: Use text blocks as
another design element 52

Tag a Terrific Page: Place a support photo on
a decorative tag 54

*Fast and Easy Stitching: Whether by hand or machine,
stitching pulls a layout together* 56

Give Support to a Support Image:
Showcase second photos with decorative frames. 58

Come Closer and Enjoy the Detail: Include "big
picture" and detail shots 60

Watch Them Come, Watch Them Go:
Show the perspective of front and behind 62

*Distressing Elements for a Well-Loved Feeling:
Sanding, inking and distressing photos and papers
for an aged look.* 64

Color or Black-and-White? Both! Create pages with
photos in black-and-white and living color 66

Intrigue With Insets: Set a photo within a photo. 68

*Fast and Easy Dimension: A little bit of depth means
a lotta dynamite.* 70

Scrapbooking With Three or MORE Photos   72

Build a Wall of Photos: Line them up for full impact. . . . 74

Show Serious Action with a Photo Series: Show action
unfolding with photo after photo 76

A Montage of Momentous Photos: Layer photos and
embellishments for an artful effect. 78

*Lace and Tie Your Pages: Fibers are fun and
funky. Find out why!* 80

The Focal Point, the Detail and the Big Picture:
Use an assortment of photos to show perspectives 82

Show Multiple Personalities: Scrapbook different
aspects of your favorite people 84

Tell the Whole Story: Design a photo essay like the pros   86

Focus on Parts of the Whole: Pull out important
details with support photos. 88

*Add Texture to Titillate: Make it nubby, make it satiny,
make it terrific.* 90

Go Big on Detail With Smaller Images: Use a slew of
images on a page. 92

*Fast and Easy Chalking: Dust off a favorite childhood
colorant for dazzle and dimension.* 94

Index. 96

Start Scrapbooking Today
Get the tools. Get the design tips. Get organized.

Fast and easy. Wouldn't it be nice to apply those two descriptive words to all of life's challenges? While noone has figured out a way to make, say, buying a house or paying off debt a carefree activity, this book holds the key to simplified scrapbooking. Not only is the book brimming with fantastic ideas for transforming your memories into finished scrapbook pages in a zip, it is organized to provide great layout ideas based on the number of photos you wish to scrapbook on a page.

In addition, you will find ten handy technique sections sprinkled throughout the book. Each two-page section tells you everything you need to know to successfully execute a popular scrapbooking technique, such as stamping or chalking. Each section features a variety of applications, and each technique has step-by-step instructions.

Got a few minutes? Get ready. Get set and get scrapbooking your favorite photos. Our talented artists will supply the inspiration while you supply your own creative twists that make your scrapbook artwork a pleasure to share with those you love the most.

Amberlee Batchelor

The Tools of the Trade

All hobbies require an investment in basic supplies and tools and scrapbooking is no exception. Here are the "must haves" you'll need to get started.

Paper

There are a dizzying selection of papers from which you can choose. When picking papers, be sure they are acid- and lignin-free to prevent deterioration, and harm to your photos.

Adhesives

No matter what you need to stick to your page, there is an adhesive guaranteed to get the job done. Invest in a glue pen (for hard-to-reach places), an all-purpose tape runner and a bottle of strong-bonding wet adhesive. Be sure the adhesives are of archival quality.

Albums

Spend time to select the right album for your project. Look at the binding—can you add more pages if necessary? Will it hold up against dust and sunlight? Is the album size too big, too small or just right? Be sure any album you buy is PVC-free, of archival quality and photo-safe.

Colorants

Colorants spice up pages. Scrapbookers use chalks, pens, markers, stamping inks, acrylic paints, pigment powders, colored pencils and more to add colorful zing to pages.

Cutting Tools

A craft knife and a trusty pair of scissors will get you started. As you increase your scrapbooking supplies purchase scissors for fabric as well as decorative scissors for cutting paper. A paper trimmer is a terrific investment for cutting long, straight edges.

Design Pointers

You could be the best photographer in the world but if you don't know how to design a scrapbook page, your images and memories will lose impact. Scrapbook page design is simple if you follow a few basic rules and learn a few helpful tips. Look at the page below to find out what makes a great scrapbook page.

Shelia Doherty

Why This Page Works: 5 Reasons

1. The focal photo is engaging. The child's open and excited expression immediately draws the eye. Star accents on the photo corners help guide the eye and hold it for a moment.

2. The colors convey the correct energetic mood. The strong primary scheme is bright and playful. The hints of red help enhance the red of the model's shirt.

3. The design shows movement. The repetition of certain elements in this design gives the page bounce. Pops of red dance around the page; star shapes anchor and accent.

4. The title is appropriate and well-executed. The vertical orientation of the title offers a unique spin on more conventional horizontal placement. Spot color is a sound choice for added accent.

5. The journaling tells the whole story behind the page, which builds a strong connection between the reader and the layout.

Organization Tips

Efficiency is the key to quick-and-easy scrapbooking. When you know where all of your supplies are, when they are organized in a logical manner and within easy reach, scrapbooking becomes much more fun. Below are some organization tips for your most common supplies.

Photos

If you organize but one scrapbooking-related item, make it your photos. This ensures that precious photos do not get damaged or, worse, lost. Be sure to give yourself enough time to tackle this job, and designate a space (away from fluctuating temperatures and direct light) where you can spread out and leave the mess for a few days. Start sorting photos chronologically. Once that is accomplished, further sort photos by theme, if desired. Place organized photos in archival-quality envelopes and boxes.

Paper

A paper collection can be separated into four categories: cardstock, patterned, specialty and scraps. Once separated, subdivide categories according to color or theme. Paper can be placed in storage drawers, hanging file folders or standing racks.

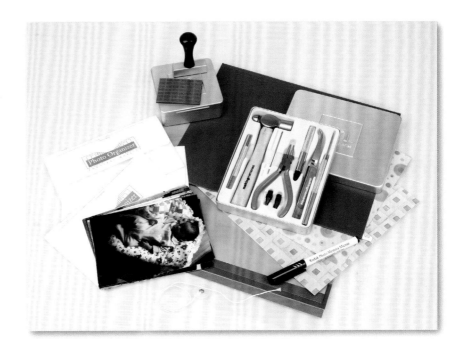

Tools

When organizing your tools, keep those that you use most within easy reach. The less you strain to find the right tool, the less body stress you'll experience. Organize lesser-used tools according to function and stow elsewhere.

Set Up a Workspace
Tips for creating a space conducive to quick cropping

- Ensure your work surface is sufficiently roomy. Give yourself enough space to spread out materials and papers.
- Keep frequently used supplies within easy reach.
- Invest in a comfortable chair with sufficient lumbar support.
- Install task lighting to reduce eye strain.
- Encourage movement by creating different work areas, such as a stamping station or a computer station. Staying seated in one position too long is not good for your body.
- If space is at a premium, utilize vertical space for storage. Just be sure to keep frequently used supplies within reach.
- Keep a trash can close by and clean between projects.
- Personalize your space with scented candles, music or creative memory art. Photos of loved ones will keep you inspired to preserve precious memories you create with them.

Scrapbooking With One Photo

It's happened to all of us—we take dozens of photos of an event and only one captures the moment as beautifully as we envisioned. Suddenly that piece of clean cardstock we'd set aside for scrapbooking this event seems to stretch for miles in all directions. You may be tempted to set that special single image aside, believing that it can't possibly hold its own on your scrapbook page. Wrong! Single-photo pages can be incredibly powerful!

There is a wide range of ways to scrapbook single photos. The key is in the quality of the picture, layout and design. We've collected some terrific single-image pages to open your eyes to the possibilities. Use these masterpieces to jumpstart your creative imagination and then make the pages uniquely your own.

Lisa Risser

Fill 'er Up With a Photo
Make the Most of One Large Image

One photo may be all your scrapbook page requires if your photo is powerful enough. Strong photos must be technically on-target, in focus, well-composed and demonstrate good tone. The photo should evoke a smile, a sigh or another strong emotion from the viewer. When you have a photo this terrific, scrapbook it on a page that allows it the room it needs to make an impact.

A mother teaches her children about life . . .

helping them to understand the **BLACK & WHITE** of life . . . the rights and wrongs . . . the good and bad . . . the ups and downs

Children return **COLOR** to their mother's life because she relearns the ability to see the blue of the sky, the depth of the oceans, and the limitless possibilities the world has to offer . . .

Margie Oliveira

Black and White and Color

This page shows a family immersed in sharing a moment as well as their gifts and insights: Parents teach children the rights and wrongs of life (black and white) and children teach parents to see the world through their eyes (color). This oversized photo is scrapbooked on patterned papers. Journaling blocks slant across the upper and lower corners. Delicate charm bracelets embellish.

Make the Most of Your Photos

Use your software to creatively alter your photo to underscore the message you wish to convey. In the photo above, the mother's image has been altered to black-and-white in order to support the page title and journaling. Using image-editing software, the artist duplicated the color photo and converted the duplicate to black-and-white. She layered the colored image on top of the black-and-white image and used the eraser tool to remove the color from the one body.

Oh That Face!

Oh that face could make a mother's heart melt! And this layout idea makes scrapbooking a single photo of a child super quick and easy. The oversized image is scrapbooked on black and white papers that are distressed with white and black inks. A stamped title, office clip and tiny tag complete the layout.

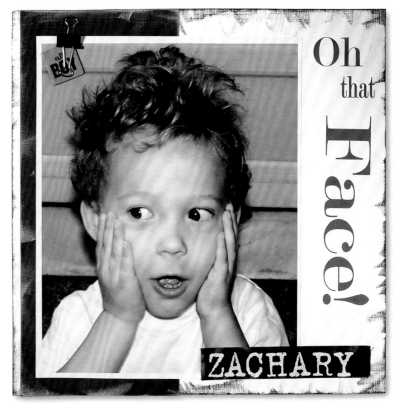

Cheryl Baase
Photo: Danielle Robertson

Randi Lanz
Photo: Sarah Tyler

Make the Most of Your Photos

Give your subjects a golden glow with backlighting. Simply place your subject in front of the light source (early morning and evening or filtered afternoon light is best), turn on the "fill flash" function on your camera and snap away. The light coming from behind will emblazon your subject and the fill flash will reduce shadows.

Hope

This beauty is even more stunning when featured in an oversized photo that is cropped so tightly you can see every strand of backlit silky hair. The image is balanced with a meaningful journaling block, tiny tiles, ribbon and a delicate title.

13

Divide and Conquer
Fill Half Your Page With a Terrific Image

Find a happy compromise by splitting a scrapbook layout 50-50 between a photo and the rest of the page. The half-and-half page format allows you to feature that oversized photo while still having room for journaling blocks, creative title treatments and embellishments. By nature, the divided page is balanced and beautiful.

Shelly Boyd

Country Girl

She's a little bit country and a lotta bit girl! This young beauty is enjoying the feel of grass between her toes. The vertically cropped image is scrapbooked on a page of interestingly combined patterned papers, a rub-on word title and a tiny flower embellishment.

Make the Most of Your Photos

When selecting patterned paper to complement your photo, choose a pattern that strongly reinforces your theme. The red-and-white gingham pattern of the red paper on the page above screams "picnic tablecloth."

Boy

Boy oh boy, this page is all about the photo. Or maybe it is about the stitching. Maybe it is about both! Stitched papers and a stamped title add elements of warmth to the vertical black-and-white picture. Little else is needed to make this page a winner.

Renee Hagler

Rebecca Swayzee

Field of Dreams

This young ball player knows what he wants, and that's a chance at bat! In the meantime, he'll wait patiently for Mom to take his photo (just as she has every year that he's played). The image is balanced by a substantial journaling block that reads, "The other day we went to the park and I watched you as I have so many times before. You were running around the play structure and every so often you would stop and slide. I was a little curious and I asked what you were doing, you said, 'I'm running around the bases and sliding home.'"

15

Fast and Easy Color Blocking
Use Paper Blocks to Create Intriguing Backgrounds

Color blocking is the process of creating a background with blocks of color. Color-blocked backgrounds can be super simple (two blocks of colored paper on a piece of background paper) or spiced up with a hint of embossed paper. Add fun accents, such as eyelets and brads, or soften the blocks with curved edges.

Accented Blocks

To begin building this color-blocked background, the artist chose the high-contrast color combination of orange and blue. She then added pastel shades into the mix. After building the background on a sheet of black paper (note how the artist left small gutters of space between the blocks, which allowed the black to peek through and provide definition), the artist added fun star accents to give the layout energy.

PAGE TOOLS & SUPPLIES

Background paper • Two or more sheets of complementary solid and/or patterned papers • Ruler • Craft knife • Accents as desired

Kelly Goree

Choosing Colors for Your Layout
ANSWER THESE QUESTIONS TO PICK NO-FAIL COLORS FOR YOUR PAGES.

- What colors are in the photo? Pick a secondary or tertiary color from the photos on which to base your color-blocking combination.
- What emotion do you wish to convey? Be sure the colors you choose thematically support the mood of your layout. If the colors in the photo clash with the mood you wish to convey, consider converting the photos to black-and-white.
- What colors are flattering to your subject? Typically, blues and oranges work well for skin tones, but experiment!
- How do you want the page to feel—open and bright or warm and cozy? For the former, opt for lighter pastels, cool tones and neutrals; for the latter, pick bolder, warmer colors.

Patterned-Paper Peekaboo

One very simple but very wowing way to enhance color blocking is to punch out a design with a paper punch in solid paper and layer it over patterned paper. Here, the artist used an "anywhere" punch to create a starburst on one of her blocks of paper. The delicate holes allow a hint of the patterned paper underneath to shine through.

I love this picture because it is so typical of how I see you. Since the day you were born, you have such a shining personality - always happy, always sparkling - and you completely entrance those around you. Your glow flows freely from your sweet face and smile and I count it among my greatest blessings that you save a lot of those smiles just for me. I love you, sweet boy. Shine on.   March, 2006

you sHine

Kelly Goree

How to Color Block
IT'S SUPER EASY TO ADD A DASH OF SASS TO LAYOUTS WITH COLOR BLOCKING.

1. Sketch layout design and cut blocks of paper to size.

2. Using an anywhere punch, create a starburst on the title block. Add title letters, handwritten journaling and accents.

3. Layer patterned paper block beneath starburst and adhere blocks to background.

17

Greet a Photo With a Welcoming Mat
Mat a Single Photo to Give It Weight

Matting a single photo adds to its visual power by enlarging the physical space it takes on the page. The mat also sets the photo apart from the business of the other page elements, providing an island of calm for the eye to rest upon. Scrapbook your single photos on a mat that matters.

Mary MacAskill

He Loves Me

An oversized mat can play double duty as the background to a photo as well as the background to the page title. The title incorporates the tiny envelope that came with the flowers the artist received from her husband. A stamped title and ribbon complete the layout.

Get Creative With Mats

You may wish to go the traditional route when matting your photos, but when the desire to go a little crazy hits, consider matting photos with:

- Circular coffee filters (spray first with de-acidification spray)
- Coasters
- A platform of stamped and combined shapes
- A swatch of fabric or lace
- Newspaper or magazine clippings (spray first with de-acidification spray)
- An oversized floral embellishment

If you are unsure of a material's archival quality, then only use a duplicate photo. Matting the photo first with acid- and lignin-free paper will help buffer the photo from potentially reactive materials.

First Kiss

The photo of this sharing moment could be lost against the lively background of complementary script papers if not for the unique photo mat. To create a similar striped background, stack the papers and cut them together. This will ensure that the newly formed paper strips are interchangeable. Layer the papers on a cardstock background leaving room between pieces for the cardstock to show.

Make the Most of Your Photos

A photo mat that contrasts against the page background will help pop your photo from the page. On this page, fluffy black fringe surrounds the photo on two sides. The photo-mat material texture, line direction and color contrast against the black, red and white background help to draw attention to the photo.

Christiana Buckley

Sand

It feels so good sometimes ya just gotta taste it! That's what this little guy has decided. The photo of this cute beach bum is simply matted on a rectangle of patterned paper. What makes the page so special is the clean white space surrounding the mat. Only a sticker title, a journaling caption and three tiny brads are needed to embellish the matted image.

Sometimes you just have to eat a little sand.

19

Celeste Smith

Being Framed Is a Good Thing
Frame Your Photo Uniquely

Just like wall art, scrapbook photos benefit from a creative and appropriate frame. Whether you go the traditional paper route or get a little more innovative, framing embraces your photo and draws the eye to the image. Select a frame that complements the colors in your image and contrasts with the background papers.

Bloom

The photo of this little flower is framed with journaling. The text is created with a combination of rub-ons and handwritten sentiments. Tiny flower embellishments decorate the corners of the photo, and an oversized flower reinforces the bloom theme.

Kim Hughes

Integrating Lettering Styles Into Your Design

Typography can add as much punch to your layout as color and pattern. Here are some guidelines to follow when mixing styles:

- Start a mix with three lettering styles so as not to overwhelm the eye. Add more styles if the mood of the page calls for it.
- Use rub-ons, stamped words and handwritten text to create a frame around a photo.
- Place words on the page so they are balanced and allow your eye to flow from one to the next.
- Be sure lengthy text is printed in an easy-to-read font.

just be you

Lisa Turley

Creative Frame Materials

Stretch your imagination and reach for less obvious materials for creating frames!

- Tiny pieces of china or stoneware to be used in a mosaic
- An old woven straw place mat to be cut into shape
- A beautiful linen handkerchief wrapped around a piece of cardstock
- Chain link adhered into shape on your background paper
- Silk flowers and silk leafy vines
- Linked earrings or necklaces

Materials may be of questionable archival quality. We recommend using with duplicate photos.

Just Be You

A classic picture frame can be created with paper to frame a compelling photo on your page. Free-hand cut the frame and journal around all sides before mounting it directly over your image. Add a rub-on title and journal along the bottom of your layout for a personal touch.

So Cute

This quick and easy page relies on two different patterns of coordinating patterned papers and, title words and supporting journaling to frame the photo of the grinning baby. Oversized alphabet stickers form the title, and rub-ons are used to journal. The center of the flower embellishment is accented with a brad.

Sarah Parrotta

Pump Up Your Photo With Patterns
Have Fun With Patterned Papers

Patterns keep our visual landscape lively. Whether they appear on clothing, on furniture or on our scrapbook pages, patterns inject fun and whimsey. Scrapbook paper is available in just about every pattern imaginable. Use patterned papers as backgrounds for your images or to embellish your favorite pages.

Heather Robertson

Hugs

Dots are in. (Okay, we admit it. They've never actually been "out.") And this perfect photo finds a perfect home on a background of green and white dots. Chipboard letters, tied together with thread, find new purpose as a container for journaling tags on this nifty page. The tags read, in part, "Sasha, Lauren's dog, is a great reminder of all the people and animals she loves in Ireland, and links them to her while she is far away in Alaska."

Make the Most of Your Photos

Why not let your child's stuffed animal take center stage in a photograph? Focus on the animal in the foreground and allow your child's image to support the furry-faced main character.

22

Baby Mine

How far can you push a patterned paper background? To the limit and then beyond! This slumbering baby has found a comfy spot to rest against this warm orange background layered with blocks of cardstock and an assortment of patterned papers. Edges of the blocks are decoratively cut. The faux stitching is created with a white pen. Shiny chipboard letters create the title and baby blue buttons embellish the layout.

Kelly Goree

Play!

This baby in blue is both excited and cautious about her first zoom down a slide! The striped patterned paper matches the blue and yellow bars of the slide. The blue photo mat keeps the photo from becoming lost among the busy pattern and also pops the blue from baby's cute overalls. Handwritten journaling tells the story while rub-ons applied to an inked tag spell the title. Buttons and silk flowers finish the page.

Ashley Calder

23

Consider a Different Point-of-View
Vary Your Photo Angles for Super Strong Layouts

A single-photo layout requires a super strong picture in order to work. Often the most interesting photos are taken from unique angles rather than simply head-on. Angled patterned papers, sweeping embellishment lines and bold colors make the most of these dramatic photos.

Barbara Dalton

Paris

From down below, the Eifel Tower looks so dramatic that your heart catches in your throat. This artist captured the famous building through her lens in a way that brackets it between two architecturally stunning buildings. The upward angle creates a soaring sensation that contributes drama to the image. A large paper letter, frame, ribbons, a floral embellishment and tiny block charm add their own elements to this lovely page.

Summertime

When a photo image is upside down, it draws the eye in a special way. This topsy-turvy photo is scrapbooked on a background of juicy orange cardstock. Journaling appears on a semicircle of lime green paper lined with aqua blue brads. The title is created with a combination of rub-ons, aqua letter brads and paper-clip letters. A large flower embellishment joins leathery flower brads and green rickrack to decorate the page.

Make the Most of Your Photos

Have you ever found the perfect paper accent only to realize it did not match the colors of your photos? Use the accent as a design guide to create a new one that is the perfect color. Trace the existing accent onto paper that matches your photos. Cut out the new accent and embellish as desired.

Katyrina Murphy

Flip Flops

Getting down to foot level makes perfect sense when you are photographing a pair of flip flops (or any other object set at or close to ground level, such as a pet or small child). This photo is matted and mounted on citrus striped paper that has remarkable resemblance to the flip-flops. A torn piece of paper creates a sandlike lower border for the page. A die-cut title is supported by colorful sticker words framed in pink book-plates. Stitched buttons add a playful touch.

Beth Sears

25

Fast and Easy Stamping
A Few Stamps and Inks Equal Hundreds of Layout Possibilities

If the number of stamps and inks on the stamping aisle of your local scrapbook or craft store stresses you out, remember this lovely acronym: K.I.S.S.—Keep It Super Simple! All you need are a few basic supplies to open the door to a world of stamping possibilities. Stamps can be used to create titles, spiff up journaling, transform plain cardstock into background paper and more.

his smile comes naturally, as does hers. she is his world, and he is hers. fatherhood comes naturally to him. without her, his smile would not be as bright, without him she wouldn't sleep at night. he is her everything, and she is his life. it just comes naturally...

Julie Johnson

Custom Background

Background stamps—big block stamps with a repeating motif—are a good investment. On this page, the artist used a few different background stamps to create a personalized background. She gathered her stamps, plus a mix of solid papers in a springy color scheme, and stamped a different motif on each color of paper. She trimmed the papers into blocks and adhered onto a piece of solid cardstock. This is an excellent way to use up some of that scrap paper!

Julie Johnson

FIRST-TIME STAMPER'S SHOPPING LIST:

Brown and black pigment ink • Watermark ink • 2 dye inks in favorite colors • Mini ABC stamp set • Basic background stamp set (geometrics, textures or florals) • Stamp cleaner

Paper Frame

A solid sheet of cardstock and a background stamp make it easy to create a custom frame or mat. Simply stamp the motif onto solid paper and either adhere your photo on top or cut out a window to create a frame.

Floral Border

To capture the spirit of this small fairy, the artist decided she wanted to create a layout free of structure and form. The resulting layout is embellished only by flower accents, a chipboard title, journaling block and a stamped photo frame.

It wasn't until you and Hayden were born that I really paid attention to the fact that everyone seems to have a nickname in our family. Your grandmother says it's just a southern thing. We have a Tootie, JC, Julie Seashore, DJ, Pamela Pearl, Lindsey Lou, Tootie, and now Bodine...

Audrey Christine is your given name. When you were little, your uncle D (again, another nickname) started calling you Audrey Bodine. Why, I have no idea. It was cute, but I never thought it would stick.

Now, five years later, you actually go by this name! It's so cute when someone asks you your name and you proudly say "Audrey Bodine."

Bodine

Julie Johnson

How to Stamp

INK. PRESS. PULL AWAY. ALLOW TO DRY. COULD IT BE ANY EASIER?

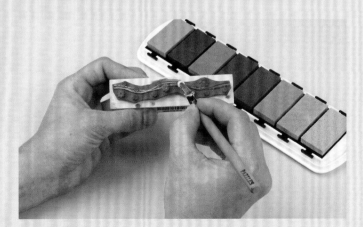

1. Using a cotton-tipped applicator, evenly apply ink to the stamp with a tapping motion.

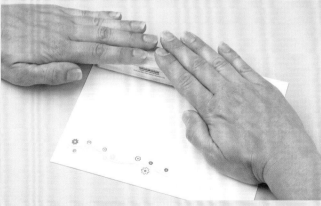

2. Place the stamp onto cardstock in the desired location and apply firm, even pressure (do not rock the stamp). Embellish stamped designs with rhinestones.

Embrace the White Space
Have Fun Scrapbooking on Clean White Backgrounds

With all of the beautiful patterned papers and glorious colored cardstocks on the market today, it takes restraint and a keen eye to know when to leave them on the shelf and instead opt for a clean, white background. Strong photos can appear even stronger when they aren't competing against other loud page elements.

BOTH THE BOY AND THE POPSICLE! JULY 2005

Celeste Smith

Delicious

The contrast between the clean white spaces and the lively colored patterned paper blocks causes this photo to jump right off the page. The artist grouped the blocks with the photo, allowing them to act as one element. She made the most of the white space by placing the element in the lower right corner. A thin border of color around the page perimeter echoes the color in the title, giving the page a finished look.

The Pluses of Scrapbooking on White Backgrounds

Yes, color is fun! But there are times when putting away the colored papers makes creative sense.

- White backgrounds work with all photos without competing with the colors within the image.
- White backgrounds allow total freedom when selecting colors of complementary page elements.
- White backgrounds contribute to pages that never look dated and always look classy.
- White backgrounds tend to visually disappear, allowing the photo to become the solo center of focus.

Wonder Boys

When a white background is mounted on top of black, the result is a layout with dimension. The black recedes and the white moves forward visually. The black-and-white photo on this page seems to move even closer to the viewer. Bright colored ice tiles, a page turn and yellow brad bring color and energy to the layout.

You Are Amazing

Clean white space makes this delicate little girl seem even more demure. Gentle pastel patterned paper creates a single strip on the lower portion of the page. Pastel coaster die cuts repeat the flower theme on her dress, and a rub-on title completes the simple but effective layout.

my wonder boys

brothers

Celeste Smith

You Are Amazing
I love you

Kim Musgrove

Make the Most of Your Photos

What is she feeling? What is she thinking? Sometimes a photo that keeps us guessing is the most interesting to scrapbook. It engages the viewer. Even after the page has been turned, an image that holds a mystery compels us to return for another look.

Clear Away the Clutter
Set Your Photo on Simple, Sleek Backgrounds

Don't 'cha just love stickers? die cuts? colorants? fibers? ribbons? stamping? YES!
But that doesn't mean that every page has to include all of those wonderful creative
supplies. It's to some photos' best advantage to be scrapbooked on simple layouts
that emphasize the photo and journaling rather than the technical skill range of
the crafter.

ABSOLUTELY ADORABLE
The "A" Man

Sometimes you are so absolutely adorable
that it takes my breath away. I can not believe
that your father and I created this truly
delectable little person. You are also such a
cool kid funny, warm, and well behaved. The
"A" Man.   September 2005

Celeste Smith

Make the Most of Your Photos

A black-and-white image always
looks classic, but a simple background showcases this quality very
strongly. While frills and froth may
come and go as styles change, a
tidy and well-constructed ensem-
ble stays in style forever.

Adorable

The color and texture of the papers
used on this layout pack a punch
while subtle details add pop. The
journaling is printed directly on
the yellow cardstock in a clean
font. A scrolled monogram letter
"A" sets up the theme for the "absolutely adorable" page.

That Sweet Face

Midnight blue cardstock is a less harsh substitute for black and better complements the soft skin tones of children. The expanses of textured blue cardstock on this digital layout recedes, allowing the photo to visually move forward. The lavender accent color is picked up in the cardstock block. A charm dangling from a tiny safety pin and flower embellish.

Angela Spangler

Secrets

Shhhhh. This little girl has something important to say. The fantastic photo is scrapbooked on pink cardstock. Decorative paper is used to create an embellishment strip and photo corner. A vertical title and journaling run up the left side of the photo while a massive flower settles in the lower page corner.

Yolanda Williams

Juggle a Photo With Colorful Paper Shapes
Use Pretty Paper to Draw Attention to Your Photo

Cut them into squares, triangles, strips or any other shape you want. Layer them, spread them out or create patterns. Any way you do it, patterned paper portions can make your background even more interesting. Select colors that speak directly to the mood of your page. Limit your embellishments and you'll be amazed at how perfectly and quickly your layout is completed.

You are one lucky girl... you are blessed with your Dad's eyelashes. They are not only long but also plentiful!

Although your hair is lighter than Dad's, your eyelashes are dark in color just like his. They naturally curl and frame your stunning hazel eyes.

I know at 6 years old you don't appreciate this, but someday you will. When you are a teenager you will realize how lucky you are!

Dawne Carlisle

Eyelashes Courtesy of Dad

A stunning cobblestone background of rounded squares mounted on teal cardstock surrounds this engaging sepia photo. Create a cobbled background quickly and easily by using punches to cut the desired shape from patterned paper. You may use a collection of identical die cuts or stickers to achieve the same effect. Fibers wind around several of the squares and a flower embellishes another.

Make the Most of Your Photos

Photo subjects needn't always be staring directly into the camera's lens to create a compelling photo. Snap photos of your subjects while they are looking down, deep in concentration, or looking up, swept away by a daydream of clouds.

Blocks

A sweeping wave of patterned paper borders the bottom of this terrific page, adding a nice contrast and very cool note to the geometric block theme and page design. Letter blocks for the title are created with letter stickers. A Dymo label and terrific journaling block underscore the story.

Wendy Inman

Sweet

Stripes made of paper result in a wonderfully easy and interesting page background. Strips of coordinating papers are inked around the edges for added appeal. Sticker letters form the title, and a tiny cluster of flowers decorates the photo corner. The apricot background paper adds warmth to the black-and-white photo.

Jacquelyne Clark
Photo: Babycakes Photography, Jennie Murphy

Fast and Easy Heat Embossing
Who Thought That Heated Powder Could Be So Cool?

Heat embossing is a great way to add a little shimmer, shine and dimension to an accent or lettering. But its touch needn't always be so subtle. You can also create negative impressions by stamping into heated powder or emboss a stamped design to resist a color wash.

A Definite Impression

Think of this as reverse embossing. Instead of stamping and then covering the image with embossing powder to be heated, the artist first created a puddle of liquid by heating a pile of embossing powder and then stamped into it. It is important to remember to first ink the stamp with pigment ink to prevent the heated embossing powder from sticking to it.

Laura McKinley

PAGE TOOLS & SUPPLIES

Regular embossing powder (as opposed to very or ultra fine powder or embossing enamel) • Pigment ink (clear, embossing or the same color as your chosen powder) • Stamp (if applicable) • Heat gun • Tweezers • Tray or small container to work in

Irresistible Resist

A resist image is created when part of a design is covered and then colorwashed. The covered part of the design "resists" the colorwash. For this coaster, the artist embossed stamped designs using clear ink and clear embossing powder. She then painted over the design in pink. The embossed images resisted the ink to create the white designs.

34

Laura McKinley

Glossy Letters

The most commonly executed embossing technique is embossed lettering. Embossing lettering, such as a title or keywords in a journaling block, gives the letters a little extra somethin'. This artist covered chipboard letters with pigment ink by swiping them across the ink pad. She then sprinkled them with clear embossing powder and heated.

Laura McKinley

How to Heat Emboss

A little ink, a little powder, a little heat and a stamp are all you need to emboss.

1. Using pigment ink, stamp an image onto the background.

2. Cover the image with embossing powder and remove excess by lightly tapping.

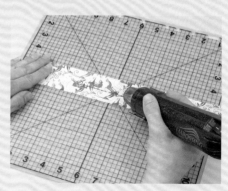

3. Apply heat until the powder is smooth and shiny.

Focus on the Face
Use a Close-up of Your Subject for Personality Pages

It is said that the eyes are the window to the soul. So if you want to truly capture the unique essence of your subject, move in for a close-up picture. Close-up photos are mesmerizing in their intimacy. Keep your page simple to prevent distractions from the image.

Paula Gilarde

Blue Eyes Mesmerize

Page elements, such as a border or, in this case, part of the title, can be used to visually crop a photo. The artist ran a strip of printed twill along the bottom quarter of the page, which allows the reader to focus on the photo subject's eyes as well as to prevent the page design from becoming static.

A

The close-up image of this little doll is featured on a background of earth-tone textured cardstock. Strips of coordinating cardstock, patterned paper and rickrack form a lower page border. The large title letter and page corner are made from mossy green papers. A flower, handcut from patterned paper, that is layered and adorned with an oversized button embellishes the page.

Nicole Stark

You Are All Girl

Pastel papers are layered to create a delicate background for this photo featuring a little beauty. Descriptive word plaques draw the eyes to the photo and add a hint of shine. The title is a combination of handcut letters and glitter stickers matted with cardstock. A tiny paper flower accent is surrounded by tiny punched holes. A larger silk flower adds balance to the oversized image.

Heather Dewaelsche

Take Better Close-Ups

Anyone who has had a camera thrust toward her face and has been ordered to "smile!" knows how intimidating that can be. For more natural results, keep the following tips in mind:

- Use a zoom lens. Stand away from your model and snap your picture from a distance.

- Enlarge a full-body photo and crop in closely on the model's face. Your photo will appear exactly as if it were taken as a close-up.

- Use soft or diffused natural light when taking photos of people.

- Be nice. Demanding "Keep your eyes OPEN" or "Smile, darn it!" only results in tears, squints or cheesy smiles.

- Engage your subject in interaction as you are getting ready to take the photo. Posed close-up shots often end up looking plastic and stilted. You'll do much better with a less formal setup.

Seize the Moment With a Tight Crop
Move in Close, Close, Closer for Terrific Photos

How close is too close? That's hard to say. But when the photo is truly wonderful, it is unlikely that you'll go wrong if you enlarge the print and crop in on the tiniest detail. Let the subtle coloration of those flower petals, the pink in your child's cheeks or the butterfly on her nose carry the emotion on your scrapbook page.

Wendy Inman

My Punkin

Cropping in close is a great way to isolate the most important details of an image. Here, the artist zoomed in on the model and his pumpkin. A waving strip of earth tone patterned paper against a textured brown background is all this page takes to be a success. The photo corner matches the die-cut letters and darker background paper. A tiny flower embellishes the lower right corner.

Make the Most of Your Photos

Whether zooming in or moving physically closer when photographing a close-up shot, be careful that you do not block the light source. Light is a very important factor in photography, but especially important for close-ups. Also, be aware of the minimum focusing distance of your lens. If you get closer than your camera allows, the resulting image will be blurry.

Seeing Eye to Eye

The chances of a butterfly landing on a child's nose at a time when you have your camera and are ready to take a photo is just about impossible. But if you are lucky enough to capture a photo of nature at work, crop in and in and in until your entire image features the nosy insect. This artist scrapbooked the photo on a background of inked patterned papers and hid a journaling block behind the photo. Tiny flowers with green brads add dimension.

Debbie Webster

Precious Jewel

Those hands are so expressive that a page title seems almost unnecessary. By cropping in tightly on the child's hands and face, the artist conveys a sense of sweet shyness and innocence. Punched circles from patterned papers form a page border. The journaling is created with a variety of inks and lettering styles. Tiny ribbons add a flourish to the layout.

Carrie Postma

Stretch Creative Impact With Panoramas
Go Wide or Long to Capture More Landscape

Panoramic photos open the lens and our eyes to what often lies just beyond the border of a photo. They offer perspective and include some of nature's most beautiful sights. Scrapbook panoramic photos alone or with supporting images. You may wish to photograph the same scene from different angles and scrapbook the photos on separate pages in a theme album.

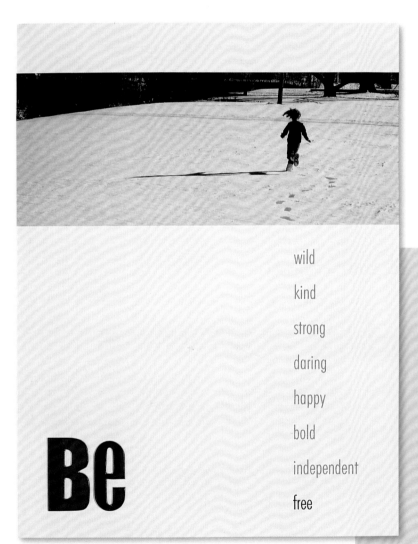

wild

kind

strong

daring

happy

bold

independent

free

Be

Teresa Olier

Be
The starkness of this layout is what makes it so stunning. The panoramic photo is run horizontally across the white background. By allowing the image to bleed off the edges of the page, the viewer is led to imagine what lies beyond the borders. Concise journaling and a one-word page title add to the clean design.

Take a Better Panoramic Photo
Panoramic images allow your camera to really open its eye (or lens) wide. Here are some ways to make the most of your panoramic shots.

- When photographing a landscape, place the horizon line in either the upper or lower third of the frame. Placing it in the middle will result in an uninteresting image.

- When including a human photo subject, frame the shot with the person left or right of center.

- Don't forget about vertical panoramas! This orientation is great for tall structures or images of standing people.

- Consider cropping 4 x 6" or 5 x 7" images into panoramas for composition with a twist.

Escape to the Sea

The beach is filled with castles or sand, heroes in lifeguard chairs and an ocean beyond which dreams lie. Escaping to the sea is a time to dream and recenter. The panoramic photo shows a sweeping view of the beach and is scrapbooked on gentle pastel papers. A vertical journaling block, fiber photo border and distressed-looking, ribbon-tied tag complete the page.

What better thing to do than pack up the cooler and head off to the beach on a Wednesday morning? I guess I'm not the typical mother because, to me, rather than send you off to the "last day of school", it's more important to spend the day watching and letting you run and play and swim at the beach. I may be unconventional, but in the end, I know I won't regret it. Although the day ended in torrential downpours, the time spent on the shore with you is something I'll never forget....

York Beach, Maine 2005

Deirdra LeBlanc

Miranda Ferski

Pick of the Patch

A photo so perfect it makes you want to set aside next weekend to visit this orchard, is scrapbooked on juicy apple colored papers. The title is created with stamps and paint. Darker colors of paint are used to outline the title letters. A definition sticker and happy grouping of ribbons complete the page.

ap·ple
(ăp'əl) n. A firm, edible, usually rounded fruit.

Scrapbooking With Two Photos

Many of the best things in life come in twos: hands, eyes, double-dip ice-cream cones and, when they are beautifully designed, scrapbook pages with two photos! There are many ways to utilize two photos on a single scrapbook page. Enlarge one and use the other as a supporting image. Use two prints of exactly the same size. Stack them, use them to balance each other, connect them with a title. The possibilities are virtually endless!

When scrapbooking with two photos, you can show multiple sides of either a personality or an event. In essence, open up the picture and allow the viewer a chance to gain a much better perspective. Select photos that share similar colors so they won't fight your choices of background papers and embellishments. Or turn one of your photos (or both photos!) black-and-white using image-editing software. No matter what your choices, you're likely to have twice as much fun!

You Are All My Heart.

turning 5

striving

seeking

I love you

[may] 2005

Callie Bug

Julie Johnson
Photos: Angie Head

Equal Rights
Scrapbook Photos of the Same Size

When you have two photos that are equally strong, it's fun to scrapbook them side by side. Stack them in any way you wish or place them shoulder to shoulder. Complete the layout with embellishments, a title or journaling block. Have fun with patterned papers or manipulate your images for extra pizazz.

Charity Hassel

Sweet Adorable Happy Faces

Lively purple patterned paper holds these two matted photos of two children. To create the flower accents, cut leaves from pieces of coordinating papers. Accent a flower embellishment by adding seed beads to the center and use fibers to create Spanish moss on tree adornments.

Lisa Turley

Homework

Photos of this young student and her chosen subject of study are scrapbooked next to each other on a layered collection of complementary patterned papers. Fun, brightly colored brads separate words along the upper photo border and on either side of the title. A handwritten journaling block tells the story of the girl's scholastic accomplishments.

What More Could I Ask For?

Image-editing software is used to make these two pup pictures look digitized, adding to the textural appeal of the page. All elements appear distressed, from the green cardstock background to the red journaling blocks. Patterned-paper page corners embrace three sides of the layout while a handwritten and painted title appears in the fourth. Tiny painted stars and strips of ribbon embellish the artwork.

Minimalist Scrapbook Pages

In design, less can be more. Challenge yourself to create scrapbook pages with only photos, papers and pens. Here are some creative ways to use your pens:

Funky frames Scribble, doodle, write words or draw lines around photos with one or two colors of pens.

Doodle Spice up mats and backgrounds with cute hand-drawn doodles of flowers, people or decorative lines and shapes.

Lots of journaling Write the journaling all over the page for a raw, artistic look.

Color block with markers Use a fine-tipped pen to outline simple geometric shapes and color them in with markers.

Christina Buckley

45

The Large and Small of It
Scrapbook With Photos of Different Sizes

When you have a photo that demands attention, print it large and use a smaller photo to support that main image. Scrapbooking two photos of different sizes allows you to include both a close-up of your model and a wider shot full of detail. There are many ways to design a big-and-little photo page. Here are three great ideas to try.

Karen Buck

True Blue

A wide strip of orange patterned paper creates a border for this so-cool-it's-hot layout. The large and small photos are joined at their inside corners. The title ties the images together while the journaling block balances the layout. Tiny blue brads and two colors of hot rickrack embellish the page.

Charity Hassel

My Hero

Childlike patterned papers form the background for this clever page. The primary photo is sectioned with a strip of paper and the rub-on title. Epoxy stickers and tags embellish the upbeat layout.

Make the Most of Your Photos

When designing a scrapbook page around an enlarged photo of exceptional proportions, consider "cropping" the photo with a strip of paper. In "My Hero," the artist ran a strip of paper along the bottom third of the photo. It helps break up the image, adds movement to the page and ties the image in to the overall design.

Sarah Sweetness

Acrylic paint dry brushed onto white paper and cut into strips decorates this simple but effective layout. The photo edges of the large and small images of the sweet-faced girl are also painted. A handcut title, journaling block and tiny ribbons add to the layout.

Rebecca Bollman

What Are You Looking At?
Combine Photos That Show Who Is Looking at What

What a wonderful idea! Why not create a page with one photo showing the model and another showing the object that has captivated her attention. Crop the two photos in any size and shape that works with your design concept. Frame them, mat them or mount them directly on your background.

The View From Our House

The young girl featured on this page simply loves the view of horses that can be seen from her back yard. The journaling at the bottom of this great page details the reasons. The panoramic photo of the horses is mounted across the lower section of the page. Sticker and rub-on letters are used to form the title.

Lisa Turley

Linda Garrity

Wonder

Delicate patterned paper and cardstock create a calm background for this pensive photo. The focal image of the young boy conveys his mesmerized state as he watches the swans. The support photo of the bird is framed within a circular window. Sticker and stamped letters as well as computer printing compose the title and journaling. A stretch of ribbon adds a pop of blue color to the top of the page.

i cannot recall a moment of my life when i didn't love the very thought of the beach. Winter, Spring, Summer or Fall. Sunrise, noon, sunset, or late at night. i love to just be there. i close my eyes and listen. i hear the ever moving waves, but i can also feel the slow deep crashing heartbeat of the ocean... of the world.

feel

"My soul is full of longing for the secrets of the sea, And the heart of the great ocean sends a thrilling pulse through me."

Roberta Lander

Make the Most of Your Photos

Inking the edges of photos adds tremendously to a layout by defining the images and giving the page more dimension. Ink the edges of your journaling and title blocks to create continuity on your page.

Feel

This child is fascinated by the feeling of water on her toes and sand beneath. Images of her contemplating both feet and water are reproduced, cropped and layered to form this digital photo montage. The journaling blocks were handwritten for a carefree beachcomber feel. Inking around elements adds yet another touch of texture.

Balancing Act
Add Poise to Your Page With a Title

Next to your photos, your title is the most important element on your scrapbook page. Deciding where to place the title can be tricky. While setting the words so they are centered in the top of the page is the obvious choice, it isn't always the most interesting choice. Consider moving your title around for some fun.

Bubble Chaser

A heavy black stamped title at the top of this page balances the colorful assortment of elements beneath. Image-editing software is used to manipulate the photos on this layout, making the images seem almost magical. Lively patterned papers form a blocked background. A green journaling tag and brad-fastened ribbons are all that is necessary to add "pop" to the page.

Strange Love

This title, created with punched circles topped with stickers, connects the two photos on the layout and creates a sense of flow. The images are matted and mounted on a collection of patterned papers. Die-cut flowers embellish the bottom of the page and join a rickrack border.

Linda Garrity

Carolyn Cleveland

Add Snap With Title Placement

There is no rule that says a title must stretch horizontally across the top of your page. Use the following title tips to create zip on your layouts:

- Run a title diagonal across a layout.
- Create a mixed-media title with leftover rub-ons, stickers, chipboard letters and more.
- Use a journaling template to create a spiraling title.
- Stack the letters of a word to create a square title.

Princess

A hand-drawn and hand-cut title runs vertically up a patterned paper background on this royally cute page. To create the superb paper embellishment, punch circles from scraps of your favorite papers. Use a black pen to define the outside edges. Adhere the circles next to each other to form flower petals around a center shape. Add a slender strip of paper for the stem and a handcut leaf.

Kim Hughes

How to Relax Your Photo Subject

While capturing a lasting image requires the right combination of light, luck and skill, the key to a really great image is a relaxed photo subject.

- Take photos of your subject at the time of day when she is most relaxed and happy.
- Allow her to lean against something, which results in more relaxed posture.
- Engage her in conversation to ease the anxiety of being in front of the camera.
- Feed her snacks so she is not cranky from hunger.
- Let her play with a favorite toy, hold a treasured object or engage in a favorite activity.

Find Balance in a Journaling Block
Use Text Blocks as Another Design Element

Journaling provides the story on a scrapbook page, so it is deserving of well-considered placement. When working with two photos, the journaling block is an excellent element for providing balance within the design. Journaling can either be short and concise or more expansive and descriptive. Have fun with words and with the style in which they are written.

Cookie

Mmmmmm. This little cookie monster is in love with his sugary treat. Photos of his cookie-eating experience are scrapbooked on a collection of patterned papers. An extensive journaling block balances the photos. Rub-on words, a stamped date, woven label and bright red brads complete the page.

Debra Hendren

Take Better Baby Photos

Those wiggling, squirming babies are as hard to photograph as cats are to herd. You'll achieve much better results if you keep the following in mind:

- Photograph babies soon after they wake. Tired babies are fussy babies.
- Take advantage of photo opportunities when they arise. Photograph your baby when he is eating, playing or otherwise involved. Don't try to clean or straighten him up. You'll only miss the moment.
- Use a zoom lens instead of trying to move in too closely on your child's face.
- Interact with your child as you photograph. Make it a happy, shared experience.

The Doctor Is In

Creative journaling fills a large portion of the upper page on this darling layout. Photos of "the doctor" and his uncertain patient are scrapbooked on patterned papers. A metal bookplate holds the proverbial red-cross symbol and a label maker is used to create journaling along the right edge of the focal image.

Amy Peterman

Beware of the Beast

Handwritten journaling fills in the areas between and beneath these two great photos. The title balances the page in areas above. Terrific patterned papers complement the theme of the reptilian page.

Alecia Ackerman Grimm

53

Tag a Terrific Page
Place a Support Photo on a Decorative Tag

Decorative tags are an excellent way to display a second photo on your scrapbook page. Tags can be created in any shape or size. They can be attached to your background with adhesive, brads or ribbon and fiber. Use the back of your tag for creative journaling!

The One With the Biggest Bucket...

This little girl is really enjoying herself in the sandbox. The oversized photo of her at play is mounted on a background of patterned paper and pink cardstock. The decorative tag holds a supporting image. Ribbons and a sticker add flair.

Slip

Cut a tag into an unexpected shape and make it the star of your layout. Here, the artist created a "before/after" feeling, but focused on the "after." The enlarged focal photo shows the photo finish of a successful slip down a backyard water slide. The photo inside the star tag shows the running start.

Robbin Wood

Kelly Goree

Ideas for Terrific Tags

Tags are an easy way to add oomph to a layout. Let these ideas inspire total tag creativity.

Accordion tag Alternately fold a strip of paper to create a small accordion tag in which to add more photos and journaling.

Altered tag Repurpose a metal-rimmed office tag by cropping support images to fit on the circular surface.

Stitched tag Add a photo to a tag and stitch the tag to your layout for homespun texture.

Snow Baby

Snow baby Ava is getting her first ride in a sled. The artist chose a bright and cheery palette based on the model's lush snowsuit. The mixed patterned paper background is enhanced with chipboard accents. The artist covered the chipboard tag frame and title block with patterned paper then sanded the edges to remove the excess.

Miranda Ferski

Dandelion

This photo tag springs up from the bottom of the layout as part of a crop of paper dandelions. The artist cut the crop from coordinating patterned papers. She cropped a photo of her son about to make a wish amidst a flurry of dandelion seeds to fit inside a circle tag created to match the dandelions. She adhered the tag to a dandelion stem with ribbon and rickrack.

Kelly Goree

55

Fast and Easy Stitching
Whether by Hand or Machine, Stitching Pulls a Layout Together

It's easy to add texture and a personal, handcrafted touch to pages with stitched accents. Stitched details can be simple—adding a crisscross stitch to the corners of a photo mat or journaling block—or more complex—stitching embellishments or adding zigzag stitches between strips of paper!

Stitch Paper Accents to a Page

Stitching is a wonderful way to secure accents and elements to a page with a decorative touch. On this page, the artist stitched around the spiral designs of the paper flowers she had cut from patterned paper. She also added a stitched border along the right side of the white paper.

PAGE TOOLS & SUPPLIES

Sewing machine • Wide-eyed needle • Thread, fiber or embroidery floss • Paper piercer

Diana Hudson

Diana Hudson

Enhance a Paper Accent

Stitched stems are a perfect way to add a little oomph to these tiny paper flowers. To add the hand-stitched stems, the artist adhered the flowers in the desired location. She then used a paper piercer to punch holes and stitched through the holes with four pieces of embroidery floss.

Stitch an Original Design

Original designs can be stitched by hand or with the help of a sewing machine. Many of today's sewing machines also come with embroidery options, which opens creative possibilities for scrapbook pages. If you are not comfortable creating your own designs, look for stitching templates at your local craft and scrapbook stores or download templates like this artist did.

Diana Hudson

How to Stitch

Down through one hole, up through the next. Stitching is very simple, but here we'll show you how to take it to the next level.

1. Download a stitching template and print it on cardstock or vellum.

2. Using a paper piercer, poke holes at the ends of the stitch marks. Cut it out, position it over your layout and pierce holes in the background.

3. Thread a needle and stitch.

Give Support to a Support Image
Showcase Second Photos With Decorative Frames

Support photos on two-picture scrapbook pages can get lost amidst patterned papers and embellishments. Make sure that your smaller photos don't suffer this fate. If they are important enough to include on a page, they are important enough to be framed! Select a premade frame or create your own with cardstock.

Julia Sandvoss

Water Play

These three are having a terrific time in the water! The primary photo is supported by a decoratively framed supporting image. Pool-blue painted cardstock and patterned papers intermingle with green page elements. To create your own bottle cap embellishments, wash and dry a bottle cap (flatten it with the whack of a mallet). Punch a circle of cardstock and adhere it to the top of the cap. Add text with rub-on letters.

Make the Most of Your Photos

Children will stay in a pool forever if you let them. For a photographer, this means that there is plenty of time to observe their interaction and fun while waiting to capture just the right joyful moment. While observing, keep an eye out for the best angle and most flattering light.

Squeeze

Before this little guy figured out that he simply wasn't going to fit through this piece of playground equipment, the artist snapped the photo! The image is silhouette cut, removing everything from the photo except the portion featured on this layout. The supporting image is seen inside a leather frame. Chipboard shapes are covered with script stickers and the extra sticker portions are trimmed away. Stickers create the title and a sticker heart embellishes the layout.

Lynnise Bowman

Make the Most of Your Photos

For a truly unique page effect, silhouette crop around a featured image using cuticle scissors. Be careful not to remove important portions of the photo (such as your model's hands!) Mount the cropped image on another page element or along the lower edge of your page.

Growing So Fast

This little cutie has something to say about the sights before her eyes. The photo in the frame shows her in full communication mode, while the primary image puts the page title in perspective. Two baby blue photo corners embrace the focal image that is matted on cheery red polka-dot patterned paper. Title letters are stamped on blocks and mounted above and below the focal image while the journaling runs vertically up the left side of the page.

Laura O'Donnell

Come Closer and Enjoy the Detail
Include "Big Picture" and Detail Shots

It's the little things that often matter, and that's why photographs of intimate details are so appealing. Scrapbook two images, one showing a wider perspective and one showing a close-up of the details involved in the activity. The closer the support image, the more impact it often has.

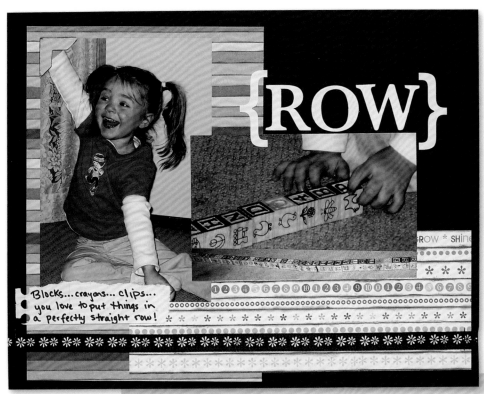

Row

Tidy rows of patterned paper strips join two terrific photos on this strong page. It is difficult to determine which of the two images is truly the focal photo. One shows the model from head to toe while the other moves in for a closer look on the project that inspires her cheery attitude. A sticker title pops off of the black cardstock background. A casually ripped corner of binder paper holds the journaling.

Rachel Cohara

Scrapbooking With Black Paper

Nothing makes color more vibrant than a black background. However, scrapbooking on a black background can be tricky. Photos and other elements often appear to be consumed as though by a black hole. When using a black background, keep these points in mind:

- Use oversized photos, when possible, to decrease the amount of black space appearing.
- Mat photos on bright or light colored papers to contrast against the black background.
- Use photos that include light backgrounds.
- Frame photos or accents with shiny embellishments or photo corners to visually lift the images off of the page.
- Run your title so that it bridges the background with your photo/s.

Slice of Summer

What's better on a hot summer day than a cool slice of watermelon? Nothing! And this young melon-eater knows that. Photos of her and her treat are scrapbooked on patterned papers against a mossy green cardstock background. The photo is double matted and mounted with a flurry of ribbons along the left side. The page is rounded off with rub-on letters, brads and wooden accents.

Lisa Turley

In and Out of Step

The powerful close-up photo on this layout shows a couple's clasped hands while the supporting image supplies an answer to the question: "Whose hands are these?" The title, created digitally, is designed to be asymmetrical to underscore the "out of step" portion of the page theme. A substantial journaling block holds its own at the bottom of the layout.

Emma Finlay

61

Watch Them Come, Watch Them Go
Show the Perspective of Front and Behind

Children are always in motion. One minute they are racing up to you for attention and approval and the next moment they've turned away to explore the world. It is fun to photograph them from the two angles and scrapbook the images on the same scrapbook layout.

Spring

A field of yellow flowers proves a perfect setting for this tyke's exploration and for the artist's photo opportunity. The image of the child from behind takes up nearly half of the scrapbook page. The title is stamped directly onto the photo. A matted journaling block is mounted next to the supporting image below.

Make the Most of Your Photos

Create a sense of distance by scrapbooking your "going away" images at the top of your scrapbook page. Scrapbook your "coming at 'cha" photos closer to the bottom of the layout.

March '03

Spring!

Every year, Mother Nature shows her true colors with the field of wildflowers near Mom and Dad's house. You, Devon, and I had just returned to the states from five months in Korea in the middle of winter. The field of yellow was a perfect welcome back to the states – the perfect welcome home.

Gwen Dye

Crawling Circles Around Grandma

A circle cutter makes perfect circles every time, which in turn makes this terrific page fast and easy. The circles are mounted to form chains with the chipboard and sticker title letters linked through the hoops. A huge flower embellishment ties together the images of this going-places little girl on the move.

Benita Coursen

Beauty

This little girl is a beauty, and so is the page displaying her coming and going photos. The entire layout is created digitally, including the patterned paper, flower accents and large stamped embellishment.

Julie Kelley

63

Distressing Elements for a Well-Loved Feeling
Sanding, Inking and Distressing Photos and Papers for an Aged Look

The word "stress" might be integral for creating the word "distressing," but anxiety certainly is not a word that springs to mind when thinking of the following techniques. Below are painless ways to add the look of vintage to your pages with a small amount of time and effort.

Distressed Paper and Fabric

This page comes alive with texture and dimension. The shabby chic patterned papers get a crumpled treatment. To crumple paper, ball a section in your hands and then flatten it out. Remove extra wrinkles by covering it with a thin cloth and running a warm iron over the top. You may wish to spritz the paper with water before ironing. If desired, run an ink pad over the top of the paper to enhance the peaks and valleys. This artist also applied ink to cheesecloth and fabric for a feathery effect. The artist coated the tile accents with watered-down acrylic paint to better match the layout.

POPULAR DISTRESSING MATERIALS:

Sandpaper • Brown and black inks • Acrylic paint • Steel wool • Bare hands for crumpling • Round-barreled pen for rolling edges • Lighter for burning paper

Laura McKinley

Laura McKinley

Sanded Edges

Sandpaper is a very popular tool for distressing. Opt for a fine to medium grade of sandpaper. For this mini album, the artist sanded the edges of the chipboard squares and also the photos. When distressing photos, be sure to use duplicate photos—a mistake could ruin a priceless treasure forever.

Distressed-Edge Effects

Layers of distressed blocks of paper give this layout a well-worn feeling. The artist began with a complementary mix of patterned papers. She then trimmed the papers into blocks to create the background and photo mats. Next, she tore the edges of the paper blocks and wrapped some of the edges around a pen to curl them.

Laura McKinley

How to Distress

Tear here. Sand there. Add a little curl. Distressing is amazingly simple.

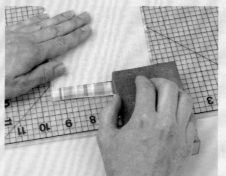

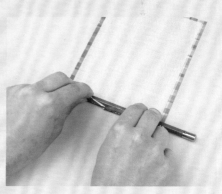

1. For a double mat, pick two sheets of coordinating paper. Trim the top mat ¼" larger than the photo. Trim the bottom layer so that the edges are ¼" wider and so that the bottom edge is ½" longer than the top layer.

2. If desired, soften the bottom edge by sanding (you can also soften it by dampening the edge). Tear the edge as desired.

3. Roll the edge toward the top by wrapping it around a round-barreled object, such as a pencil.

Color or Black-and-White? Both!
Create Pages With Photos in Black-and-White and Living Color

If you often feel you are in a creative tug of war trying to decide whether to use black-and-white or color photos, relax. You can create wonderful pages mixing the 7 coloring options on the same layout. The photos will actually complement each other and add a nice creative touch to your scrapbook art.

Norma Kennedy

I Love You

Photos document growth from year to year. Scrapbooking a photo of your child as a toddler and then again years later shows both similarities and differences. These photos are matted on coordinating papers and mounted on a warm yellow patterned paper. A bold black-and-white title, decorative ribbon and a tag complete the no-fuss layout.

I Look Just Like Mom

Scrapbooking photos from different generations of family members is a terrific way to incorporate a heritage picture with a modern image on a single layout. These photos are matted identically, but the black-and-white image lifts to reveal journaling. The bold pink title is supported with tiny tags, which are held in place with pink brads.

Julie Gelfand

Love the Moment

A focal image is matted on blue before being mounted on a cool green background on this digitally created scrapbook page. A second black-and-white image appears in whole, and in part, three different times. Digitally painted slashes and punched circles join the title and journaling to complete the layout.

Ann Hetzel Gunkel

Sparkle

Whether featured in black-and-white or full color, this little cherub shines! The focal image is matted on purple paper. Wedge-shaped pieces of the same paper border the mat, creating asymmetry that adds visual interest. The colorful supporting photo is matted on fiery orange paper. Letter stickers create the title and page embellishments while colorful brads add their own punch to the sunny layout.

Pamela Rodriguez

Intrigue With Insets
Set a Photo Within a Photo

When your main photo is strong enough to fill the page and you still want to include a supporting image, consider mounting the smaller photo directly on top of your focal picture. A scrapbook page with an inset seems almost magical. Use this technique for any theme you wish. It is easy to be successful with insets.

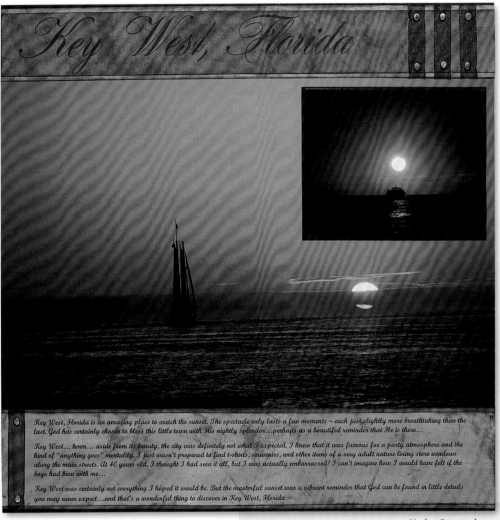

Kathe Cunningham

Key West, Florida

The spectacular focal image is strong enough to fill all the space on this layout, however the smaller inset photo adds its own appeal by creating a sense of elapsed time. The journaling block at the bottom of the page works beautifully with the color palette. The title at the top is printed on distressed patterned paper. Small brads embellish the layout.

Make the Most of Your Photos

Silhouette images are stunning and, with a little practice, easy to capture. Strongly backlit (light from behind your subject) situations result in the most dramatic silhouettes. Just remember these simple rules: The light behind the subject must be stronger than the light on the subject. Expose for the background.

Just One More Ride

"Just one more ride, Daddy, please!" While at first glance this layout looks like a carefree romp in the waves, a look at the journaling shows that this page is about gratitude. The inset on this layout shows a clearer view of a super father/son moment. The enlarged photo shows the super action and fun of the moment.

Julie Johnson

Child's Play

The land of make-believe is well-traveled by this little imagination. Normally, the inset is used to zoom in on the detail, but for this layout, the artist chose it to show the big picture. The enlarged detail shot shows adorable chubby little fingers acting out life from a galaxy far, far away.

Julie Johnson

Fast and Easy Dimension
A Little Bit of Depth Means a Lotta Dynamite

Adding dimensional accents to pages makes a scrapbook come to life. The different height levels and shadows pique a reader's interest and make her wonder how such delicate craftsmanship is accomplished. Adding dimension is easy. It can be done with premade accents or by adhering elements with foam adhesive.

Button Background

This is one easy and colorful way to add dimension to a page. The artist adhered a bevy of buttons all over the layout's background to act as photo and journaling frames. Look at your local scrapbook and craft store for self-adhesive buttons to make this job a snap.

MORE WAYS TO ADD DIMENSION

Shadow-box frame • Microbead accents • Beaded borders • Premade dimensional accents • Fiber-enhanced tags

Shannon Taylor

Making a Safe Journey Into the Third Dimension

Follow these rules of caution and care when creating dimensional scrapbook pages.

Reinforce page backgrounds If you go heavy on the dimensional accents, provide extra stability by adhering the page to a piece of foam core.

Store albums upright If you lay an album flat, gravity can take its toll and the weight pressure of dimensional pages can damage photos.

Watch out for sharp points When working with materials such as wire or some brads, be sure that the sharp points are not damaging other pages in your scrapbook.

Add room to your albums If you include several dimensional pages in your scrapbook, don't pack the album tightly. Add foam spacers to the album binding to give 3-D pages more room.

Shannon Taylor

Pop-up Paper Flowers

Foam adhesive—spongy foam that is sandwiched between double-sided tape—comes in all shapes and sizes. It's great for giving pages just a little bit of pop or a wallop of depth. For this page, the artist cut out flower motifs from patterned paper and layered them on top of each other for a bouncing flower border.

How to Add Dimension

That look of depth and dimension for your scrapbook page is easier than imagined.

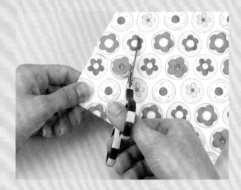

1. Trim individual flowers from patterned paper.

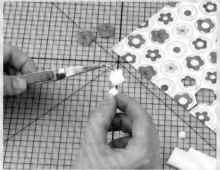

2. Adhere small squares of foam adhesive to backs of half of individual flowers cut from patterned paper.

3. Adhere small flowers to strip of paper, alternating flowers with foam adhesive with flowers adhered directly to the cardstock.

Scrapbooking With Three or MORE Photos

Three photos form a triangle, a perfectly balanced form that offers a plethora of options for the placement of other page elements. It also offers choices when it comes to the combinations of size and shape of your photos. You may decide to scrapbook three images of exactly the same dimension, or enlarge one and use smaller supporting photos. Use two photos on tags. Build a collage of images. The options are seemingly endless!

While scrapbooking with a single strong photo has its own powerful appeal, scrapbooking with three or more photos allows you to feature more images on a page. That means more photos in albums and fewer in boxes under the bed! With multi-photo pages, you can tell "the rest of the story," leaving out not one detail. So pull out those envelopes filled with pictures and group them on pages you'll enjoy for years.

Margaret Oliveira

Build a Wall of Photos
Line Them Up for Full Impact

A wall of photos forms a sort of barrier that compels the eye to stop and look. Whether stacked vertically or horizontally, a wall of photos allows the viewer to track the images easily. Scrapbook pages designed in this manner offer wide expanses of space for decorative page borders as well as title and journaling blocks.

Jake

This kitty couldn't be cuter, and stacking photos of his antics adds to the fun of the layout. The pictures are scrapbooked on a playful black and polka-dot patterned paper background. A strip of pastel striped paper supports the title, created with fuzzy alphabet sticker letters.

Raechelle Bellus

Laura O'Donnell

Fun

Get ready, get set, JUMP! These photos of the launch are mounted horizontally in a manner that resembles the frames of a movie. The black-and-white paper is inked to make it a bit more rustic. The large flower embellishment adds zing with its peppery green petals. A similar green is picked up with the photo corner and title letters.

Joy Boy

This little guy stole the hearts of his parents and that's no surprise. Three photos of him on the road to success are mounted side by side over playful patterned paper and bright orange cardstock. Rub-on words and stickers form the title and journaling. A touch of ribbon, tiny tags and an epoxy sticker embellish the layout.

Make the Most of Your Photos

When you are using striped patterned paper it can be fun and effective to mount photos at angles (rather than along vertical and horizontal lines). This little rebellious act is enough to put a creative spin on your layout.

Charity Hassel

Zany Little U

Three baby photos are matted side by side on white cardstock and then mounted on a peachy background on this delicate page. A title block of baby blue paper provides a clean platform for the rub-on and sticker title. Photo turns and delicate flowers balance the layout.

75

Ashley Cantin

Show Serious Action with a Photo Series
Show Action Unfolding With Photo After Photo

Lights, camera, action! Life seldom holds still, and that's one reason that scrapbook pages showing photos capturing action as it happens are so interesting. By using photos in this manner, you can truly zoom in on the personalities of your models through shifts in their expressions and body language.

Miranda Ferski

Little Linus

A snuggly blanket represents everything right in the world of a baby. This little guy is attached to the blanket created by his grandmother. Photos of the babe and blankie are scrapbooked from all directions on a page of pastel green patterned paper. Another block of patterned paper (blue) runs across the lower portion of the page and holds the stamped journaling block. Stenciled letters create the title. A fist full of flowers adorns the upper corner of the page, and ribbons decorate the bottom corner.

Lime

A series of seriously funny photos documents the lime-tasting event shared by these two children. The focal image is strong enough to stand up under the weight of the lime green title. A creative touch of spot color turns the lime in his hand bright green. Supporting photos are mounted horizontally and run shoulder to shoulder up the left side of the page to create a border. Journaling runs across the bottom of the layout.

Dana Swords

Competition

Will the winner be the airborne dog or the one who waits patiently for the snowball to land? The answer to the question is given in the subsequent images. The patterned paper along the left page edge provides a background for rickrack and snowflake stickers.

Pam Callaghan

A Montage of Momentous Photos
Layer Photos and Embellishments for an Artful Effect

Montage is a popular way to bring together a number of different elements in a collective design. Photos are grouped and layered on top of each other, intermingling with paper and three-dimensional embellishments. Place photos in a calculated pattern or mount them at random for a less formal effect.

Beth Root

Something Wicked This Way Comes

A collection of photos from a Halloween past are collected in the center of this page. They rest on a pile of seemingly nonchalantly tossed patterned papers. Various papers have been folded and secured with brads. A large monogram letter is decorated with ribbons, brads and typewriter letters. The title block quote from Shakespeare and other stickers create the Monster Mash journaling to form a page that makes a true statement.

Double-Sided Patterned Papers
For extra punch on your pages, use double-sided patterned papers. These specialty papers can be found in a wide selection of patterns. Here are some ideas for using them:

- Mount the paper on your page and fold back ends of corners for a dash more pattern, color and dimension.
- Create pinwheels by cutting four-pointed flowers from patterned paper. Fold in tips and secure with brads.
- Make double-sided accordion cards by cutting a strip from patterned paper and alternately folding to expose both sides of the paper.

The journaling on the image reads:

2. I love her so much I need to stop playing and give kisses

3. I enjoy pushing her around a little (not too hard!)

4. Then I stick my tongue out at her. She does the same. Funny!

5. Then we take a break for a while and think up new games.

1. There is no greater joy than playing with my best friend.

My best friend and me

Mireille Divjak

Best Friend

Five fun photos of this baby admiring her own image in a mirror are cut into circles and mounted on top of a cluster of circular pieces of patterned papers. Journaling skims along the perimeter of the papers. Flower embellishments are mounted in the center of the photo group and at the ends of ribbons, which have been slipped beneath the photos. Playful charms are secured with brads to form the centers of the flowers.

Lace and Tie Your Pages
Fibers Are Fun and Funky. Find Out Why!

Long and luxurious or cute and simple, strands of fibers, ribbons and threads beg for scrapbookers to create with them. They can provide pure decoration or put the "fun" into a functional page element. Some of scrapbookers' favorite uses for elements of the string variety include topping tags and tying tiny closures.

Tia Bennett

Folio Closure

Embroidery floss plays a small but necessary supporting role on this page. Under the energetic star and ribbon accents is found a piece of floss that, when unwound, frees an interactive page element to open and reveal journaling.

PAGE TOOLS & SUPPLIES
Fibers, ribbons and/or embroidery floss • Wide-eyed needle • Paper-piercing tool

Laced Edge

Playful ribbon hugs the edges of this mini album's photo mats. The ribbon introduces pattern, color and texture to the otherwise minimalist creation. The artist set eyelets around the perimeter of the photo mats, through which she laced ribbon.

Tia Bennett

Corset Lacing

The crisscross of corset lacing is undeniably feminine. It can add a beautiful mystique to pages. For this page, the lacing adds a lovely touch to a photo frame.

Tia Bennett

How to Lace

It's as easy as creating the switchbacks of a laced sneaker.

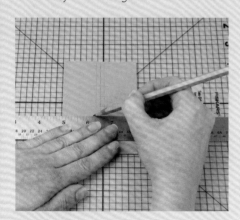

1. Trim a 3 x 4½" piece of cardstock and draw a line down the center. Draw another line ¼" from each side of the center line. Mark the lines at ½" intervals.

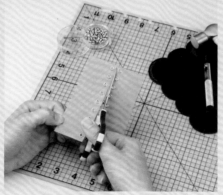

2. Set eyelets at intersections. Cut the block in half.

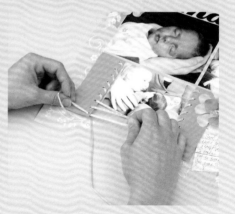

3. Attach blocks to the background in the desired location. Lace ribbon through the eyelets just as you would lace a shoe.

The Focal Point, the Detail and the Big Picture
Use an Assortment of Photos to Show Perspectives

It is a filmmaker's technique to mix together wider angles with close-ups and reverse shots. It is done so well that you seldom notice what is actually taking place. All you know is that you have a comprehensive and interesting look at the action. Use the same technique to create mesmerizing multi-photo scrapbook layouts.

How to play the Learning-to-Read-Game

Darren has very specific ideas how things should be done. For example, this is Darren's set of rules how to play the "Learning How to Read" – game: 1) Mommy holds the cards in one hand and covers the pictures with her other hand. 2) Darren reads the words on the cards. 3) Mommy puts the cards on the table. 4) Darren places the foam letters on top. 5) When Darren is finished we move on to the next set of words. And THAT is how we play this game!

Janneke Smit

How to Play the Reading Game

Look at that face! This little guy is proud of his growing reading ability and should be! The portrait, perspective photo and close-up cutaway are mounted on a terrific teal textured background. A border of patterned paper balls establishes the palette for the decorative paper strips. Tiny colored rings embellish the page.

Make the Most of Your Photos

When picking a focal photo, be sure to go for the most compelling image. Spread your photo choices out before you and give them a good look. Which photo causes you to stop and stare, smile or giggle?

Daddy's Shoes

Those shoes may be meant for walkin' but mount a few wheels on the bottom and this little cherub is more likely to use them as a skateboard! The three photos show a full body image of the child and close-ups of her over-sized footwear and her grinning face. Put the photos together on a background of sassy colored patterned papers and you've got a winning layout. A title and handwritten journaling add to the story.

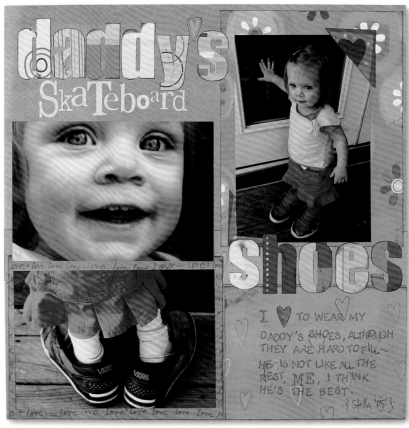

Alecia Ackerman Grimm

Paulina Soria

Turtle Pond

Turtles are so amazing, you can't help but look at them with wonder. The photos on this page are a progression of sorts. The artist says she wanted to emphasize the act of her sister looking at the turtles, so she cropped close and enlarged a photo of her sister peering over the railing. She then added the turtle photos beneath the focal photo. This digital layout shows the entire experience!

Show Multiple Personalities
Scrapbook Different Aspects of Your Favorite People

One minute she is grinning, the next pouting, the next tearing up. Emotions and expressions change as often as spring weather. And that's what makes people so interesting! Scrapbook multiple photos of a subject's personality on a page that shows how unique she is.

Amy Farnsworth

All Personality

You just have to grin at this babe. The primary photo is so terrific you might not look at the supporting photos if the large flower embellishment didn't draw your eye to the right portion of the page. More flowers embellish the left side of the layout along a rickrack trail. Title stickers and a journaling block sum up the page theme beautifully.

Make the Most of Your Photos

When your stickers or other embellishments simply don't work with your photos, change them! Use acrylic paint to alter the elements. Allow them to dry, and mount them as desired.

84

Swing

To a child, a playground is a place to test his physical abilities, courage and imagination. It is the perfect place for a photographer to capture photos of her child that convey the many sides of his personality. These photos are scrapbooked on patterned papers. The stitched patterns are created with a pen rather than thread. A rub-on title and playful fabric flowers with shiny centers completes the layout.

Make the Most of Your Photos

Shooting a close-up portrait straight-on often results in a static photo. Have your subject tilt his head, look over a shoulder, or take a profile for a more dynamic composition. Best yet, capture your model while he is engaged in an activity.

Mikki Livanos

Art of God

The photos on this all-digital page show the many sides of this youngster. She is sassy, she is mod and, above all, she is sweet. The distressed-effect pink paper and butterfly accent add a rustic touch to the layout.

Lisa Spring

85

Tell the Whole Story
Design a Photo Essay Like the Pros

A photo essay groups together terrific images to tell a story that takes place over a period of time. These essays often have a beginning, middle and end, just like any tale. Photos can be arranged in any order, but most often there is a primary photo supported by support images that tell the full story.

Debbie Hodge

First Sleepover

This little guy's expression would melt any mother's heart. The focal photo and title tell so much of the story that the supporting photos are simply whipped cream on the perfect cake. Chipboard and die-cut letters create the title. Journaling runs vertically up the page. Bold crisscross stitches join the block of patterned paper to the golden cardstock. Both papers are mounted on top of a darker brown background.

Swimming Lessons

The story of this young swimmer's success is told in a series of photos mounted on a die-cut filmstrip. The primary photo sums up the athlete's feelings about her accomplishment while the embellished envelope holds her Red Cross Level I Water Exploration Certificate. Chipboard letters are used to create the first word of the title and letter stickers spell out the rest. Journaling is typed on a torn piece of vellum and mounted at the bottom of the page.

Jill Stenglein

Make the Most of Your Photos

Professional photographers always say, "Film is cheap; it's the shot that you miss that costs the most." You need to take a lot of photos to get a good one. If film and processing costs seem expensive, then take a long-term approach and invest in a good digital camera.

8 Months

This little cutie is embarking on an exciting and very important adventure. He's learning to eat solid foods. More importantly, Mr. Independent is learning to feed himself! The process doesn't happen overnight. At first the baby can only (barely) manage to navigate large pieces of food to his mouth. And, that food seldom arrives in one piece. But before long, he's carefully plucking banana wheels from the plate and looking at that spoon with interest. This layout dedicates most of its space to the four photos. Journaling and a title sit neatly at the bottom of the page.

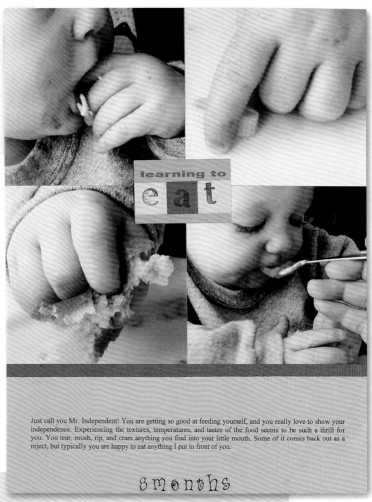

Just call you Mr. Independent! You are getting so good at feeding yourself, and you really love to show your independence. Experiencing the textures, temperatures, and tastes of the food seems to be such a thrill for you. You tear, mush, rip, and cram anything you find into your little mouth. Some of it comes back out as a reject, but typically you are happy to eat anything I put in front of you.

8 months

Kelli Dickinsen

Designing a Scrapbook Spread

While many scrapbookers enjoy creating a single-page layout, others feel that a spread gives them more room to really tell the story. When creating a two-page layout, keep the following in mind:

- Design the two individual pages of a spread as if they were a continuous whole.
- Design the layout so that the title page falls on the left scrapbook page.
- Place elements so the eye flows from the top left to the bottom right.
- Use papers, embellishments and techniques to tie the pages together—strive for continuity.
- Consider bridging the gutter between the two pages with an element, such as a title or border, that appears to continue from one page to the next.
- Place your photos so they have a natural order of progression from the left page to the right.

Focus on Parts of the Whole
Pull Out Important Details With Support Photos

When portions of a photo are especially important and your focal image does not seem to give them the up-close-and-personal that they require, use close-ups to shine the spotlight on these features. Mount the pull-outs on tags, as inserts or as supporting photos on your page.

Rebecca Swayzee

Teamwork

These pals are all for one and one for all. The photo of their connection is scrapbooked on a digital layout of beige, lime green and tomato red. Small photos of three portraits are mounted directly on the focal image within green frames. Journaling drums up a team cheer.

Make the Most of Your Photos

Sometimes the most compelling images can be taken when behind the action. In the layout above, the artist captured the camaraderie between these youngsters by photographing them from behind and thereby capturing an endearing image of linked shoulders.

Benny G

Mastering a musical instrument isn't easy. It takes focus and hours of work. This young musician is up for the challenge. Photos of his practice create a border for this page. The focal image is surrounded with fiber, a buckle and tags. Hidden journaling reads, "It brought tears to my eyes when I heard you practicing the music for 'Mary Had a Little Lamb' with your new alto saxophone. Maybe it is because as your mom, I did not have any musical talent and returned my flute only weeks after I first got it. ...Daily, you enthusiastically brought your instrument home and practiced. The 'joyful noises,' as your band director calls them, are simply beautiful!"

Jacquie Veach

Jennifer Maceyunas

Baxter and Molly

A supersized photo of Baxter and Molly is framed with torn pieces of grass green cardstock that's been mounted over the upper and lower portions of the photo. The two dogs are shown up-close in supporting photos that are matted and mounted to overlap the primary image. Letter embellishments are mixed and matched to form the title. The decorative dog collar creates a border along the lower portion of the page.

Add Texture to Titillate
Make It Nubby, Make It Satiny, Make It Terrific

Adding texture to your scrapbook page is a wonderful yet subtle way to induce nostalgia. The best place to find textural inspiration is from your photos. By mimicking a texture found in the pictures, the scrapbook page stays true to the memory and also acts as a unifying page element.

Trudy Sigurdson

PAGE TOOLS & SUPPLIES

The model's clothing • The sky, land and water • The weather • The surface of an architectural element • Food • An object, such as a bike tire • The action shown in the photo

Texture of the Feminine

Fabric is a favorite way to add texture. Because of its myriad textures and patterns, you can find a fabric to suit any texture need. This frame takes advantage of opulent fabrics that showcase the divine femininity of these three beautiful girls. The artist covered a plastic scrapbook page frame with fabric and added black satin trim to finish.

Texture of the Weather

All of the materials used for this page impart a brrrrrr! feeling. The artist wanted an icy background for the journaling. She began with self-adhesive masks (premade transparent designs used to create a resist), which she stuck to her background with temporary adhesive. She dry embossed around the designs with a stylus. She then blotted over the masks with white acrylic paint. Once dry, she removed the masks and traced the embossed outlines with glitter glue.

Trudy Sigurdson

90

Texture of the Land

The brown, rocklike texture shown behind the journaling blocks was created by layering papers with a texture medium. The artist furthered the earthen theme by inking the edges of the texturized block as well as the journaling blocks. She chose plain chipboard letters for the title because the grainy surface mimicked the rocks in the photos.

Ever since Mr Hamm started teaching at Beaver Lake Elementary School the grade 4 classes started a unit on cycling and had to cycle 100 km's with in a certain period of time. At the end of the unit Mr Hamm, along with some of the other grade 4 teachers and parents, would take the kids on a 38km bike trip around Saturna Island. On this overcast June day we all drove out to the ferry terminal, got all of the kids and bikes ready and cycled onto the ferry for the hour long trip. Once we arrived and got off the ferry we started the long bike trip started around the island. Midway through the day we all stopped at the tip of the island and had lunch. Afterwards the kids had some time to explore and walk on the beach. This beach was one of the coolest beaches I have ever seen because instead of having sand, it was covered with sandstone. Some of it was as smooth as can be, while some of it had been eroded in the most unusual way and was full of these little pockets and holes. After an hour or so on the beach it was time to get back on the bikes for the long ride back to the ferry and another hour long ride home. June 2003

Trudy Sigurdson

How to Texturize
Several ways to add texture exist. Here is one.

1. Cut a 3¾ x 1¾" piece of cream textured paper and blot it with walnut ink.

2. Cut a similar-sized piece of speckled handmade paper and lay it on top of the cream paper. Using a foam paintbrush, cover it with a layer of paper adhesive and press the papers together with the foam brush. Allow to dry.

3. Ink around the edges with a black chalk inkpad, then blot on top of the textured paper to highlight the texture.

Go Big on Detail With Smaller Images
Use a Slew of Images on a Page

You have more photos than you can shake a stick at, and you want to scrapbook ALL of them on a page! Well, put aside your concerns and get started! Select a focal image that supports your page title and theme. Creatively place your supporting photos so they tell the rest of the story.

Sonya Shaw

Jeffrey 05

A day in the life of a boy is full—very, VERY full! Creating a page that displays photos of his going-and-doing lifestyle is a terrific way to use up dozens of images. Surround the matted focal photo with the supporting pictures, mounting everything on a clean white background. Hand journal around your primary picture and add a large date directly on the primary photo's mat.

Literary Tea

A very special tea party is scrapbooked on a page filled with fun photos. The focal image is matted on patterned paper with rounded corners. Supporting photos appear as a black-and-white border on the right side of the page. The large stencil and letter stickers create the title. Below, a decorative envelope is filled with additional journaling including the tea invitation. A dollhouse picture frame, ribbons, rickrack, tea bag tags and brads decorate the layout.

Debbie Hodge

The Pulse of Freedom

Rectangles of interesting patterned papers are intermingled with photos cropped to an identical shape and size on this meaningful layout. The photos offer snapshots of an American solider's Iraq experience. Only a title and minimal journaling are needed to accent this powerful page.

Amy Teets
Photos: Jason Teets

Scrapbooking Military Memories

Photos of military service are especially important to scrapbook. They honor those who are serving their nation. But scrapbooking these photos does even more:

- It keeps children in touch with the parent who is away.
- It keeps couples united and updated.
- Consider scrapbooking a military page opposite a scrapbook page showing events taking place back home for an important historical record.

Fast and Easy Chalking
Dust Off a Favorite Childhood Colorant for Dazzle and Dimension

When it comes to chalk, most scrapbookers have plenty of experience with it, having used it as children to write on blackboards or sidewalks. Now, with a little finesse, chalk is a wonderful colorant to use to add texture, depth and soft color to scrapbook pages.

Samantha Walker

Add Definition

If you're looking for an easy way to add light-weight dimension to your page, look to chalk. By using chalk to shade the edges of page elements, you can create a shadowy effect. For this splish-splash page, the artist cut brown paper in the shape of puddle splashes. She used a cotton swab to outline the edges of the paper with brown and black. Once finished, she sprayed the chalk with a fixative spray, allowed it to dry and layered the designs on her page background.

PAGE TOOLS & SUPPLIES

Artist-quality chalks • Applicators (cotton swabs, triangular makeup sponges, eye-shadow applicators) • Fixative spray

Create a Tone-on-Tone Effect

Chalk can also be used to create an artistic tone-on-tone effect. For the cover of this album and the page titles, the artist first stamped the image and letters using watermark ink, which is clear. Once the ink dried, she applied chalk with a small cotton-tipped applicator in a pouncing motion.

Samantha Walker

Color a Background

Chalk use needn't always be subtle. Chalk can create vibrant, saturated color. This design resulted when the artist applied chalk directly to a page background with enough hand pressure to produce bold color. She used a pencil eraser to erase some of the chalk for a striped effect.

Samantha Walker

How to Chalk

Soft or bright, chalk can be applied to pages for colorful might.

1. Pick a few colors of chalk to coordinate with your photos and alternately apply them to the background with a sponge-tipped applicator or your finger.

2. To create stripes, line up a template over the chalked marks and, using a pencil eraser, remove the chalk.

Index

A

Acrylic paint 47, 84

Adhesives 7

Albums 7, 80, 94

B

Baby 23, 52, 55, 62, 63, 67, 75, 76, 79, 80, 81, 84, 94

Backgrounds 16, 17, 26, 27, 28, 32, 33, 37, 78, 90, 91, 93

Beach 19, 25, 41, 49, 54, 57, 63, 64, 68

Birthday 43, 70

Borders 39, 56, 67, 89

Bottle caps 58

Boy 6, 13, 15, 28, 30, 38, 75, 80, 92

Brads 45

Buttons 70

C

Chalk 94, 95

Colorants 7

Color blocking 16, 17, 45

Color, choosing 16

Cutting tools 7

D

Digital pages and elements 49, 57, 61, 63, 67, 85

Dimensional accents 70, 71

Distressing 13, 45, 49, 64, 65

Doodling 45

E

Embellishments 25, 53, 84

Embossing 34, 35

F

Fabric 90

Family 12, 56

Favorites 6

Flowers 36, 44, 51, 56, 71, 79

Food 52, 77, 87

Frames 20, 21, 45, 90, 92

Friends 11

G

Girl 13, 14, 20, 21, 26, 27, 29, 31, 33, 36, 37, 39, 47, 51, 83, 85, 90

Growing 59, 70, 86

Halloween 78

I

Insets 68, 69

Interactive pages 80

J

Journaling 15, 20, 39, 45, 52, 53, 66, 69, 93

L

Lacing 80, 81

Learning 82

M

Military 93

Music 89

N

Nature 39, 53, 55, 73, 83

O

Organization tips 9

P

Page-design tips 8, 14, 20, 28, 29, 30, 31, 32, 33, 36, 40, 45, 60, 62, 63, 75, 87

Paper 7

  Patterned 14, 22, 23, 25, 38, 53, 55, 75, 78, 93

  Personality 16, 17, 40, 44, 84, 92

Pets 19, 35, 45, 50, 74, 77, 89, 94

Photo essay 86, 87

Photo mats 18, 19

Photomontage 49, 78, 79

Photo tips

  Action shots 74, 75, 76, 77

  Backlighting 13

  Black-and-white 30, 66, 67

  Close-ups 37, 38, 60, 61

  Cropping 47, 55, 59

  Detail shots 60, 61, 82, 83, 88, 89, 92, 93

  Digitally altering 12, 45, 49, 50

  Panoramic 14, 15, 40

  Perspective 22, 24, 25, 58, 62, 63, 82, 83, 88

  Photographing people 29, 32, 51, 52, 58, 84, 85

  Selecting images 82

  Series 74, 75, 76, 77

  Silhouette images 68

Physical features 32, 36, 66

Play 23, 33, 50, 53, 59, 60, 69, 74, 85

R

Relationships 18, 26, 34, 47, 56, 61, 64

Ribbon 61, 80, 81

S

Seasons 34, 38, 41, 55, 61, 62, 65, 90

School 45

Siblings 29

Singing 8

Sports 15, 80, 88

Stamping 26, 27

Stitching 56, 57, 86

Stuffed animals 6, 22

T

Tags 54, 55

Texture 90, 91

Titles 41, 50, 51, 59, 89

Travel 24, 91, 95

W

Water play 46, 54, 58, 69, 86

Workspace (building a) 9